HE WAITED
for Me

SAUNDRA L. WORDS

ISBN: 979-8-9924653-0-3 (Paperback)
        979-8-9924653–2-7 (E-book)

Library of Congress Control Number: 2025901675

Published By:

Saundra L. Words

Mansfield, TX
https://www.facebook.com/leadandguideme

Publisher Provider:

~ He ~

He is <u>Alpha</u> and <u>Omega</u>

He is the one true God

He was here from the beginning and called the world into existence.

He who spoke to the winds and waves and caused them to be still.

He who set time in motion, spoke the planets into space and spotted the stars in the sky to sparkle.

He who walked on water and calmed the ragging waves.

He who is patient, kind and forgiving.

He who was crucified but rose again on the third day.

He who is a very present help in the time of trouble.

He who knew me before I was in my <u>mother's</u> womb.

He who knows every strand of hairs on my head.

He who loves unconditionally.

He who protects me when trouble is at hand.

He who heals my body.

He who blesses the righteous and unrighteous.

He who is the great I Am.

~ Waited ~

Stay where one is or delay action until a time or until something else happens. To put off, to remain or hang on.

~ For ~

On behalf of or in favor of.

~ Me ~

A Sinner

Table of Contents

Chapter One

Stubborn Child

I remember learning about Jesus and God as a young child because my Mother made us go to church. In most African American homes, you would find a picture of a white Jesus displayed in a gold colored frame hanging on the wall. My Mother was beautiful. She had smooth caramel brown skin, petite in size and stood 5 foot 3 inches tall. She worked outside the home as an Aide at the State Hospital. But when she opened her mouth to address us, it was as if God himself had given a command.

There were six children still in the home. My oldest sister was eight years older than me. She graduated from High School, married her high school sweetheart and moved away. My Mother was the boss of the children. My Father stood almost 6ft tall, thin frame and dark chocolate colored skin. He had white teeth, big round eyes and a breathtaking smile. My Father was a handsome looking man indeed! He worked as a janitor at a food supply house across the river. He was more reserved than our Mother and 99% of the time, she was the disciplinary. She would often tell us kids: "Do as I say and not as I do."

When Saturday night came, we had to have our clothes neatly laid out at the bottom of our beds. There was not going to be any excuses such as: "I don't know what to wear or I can't find my other sock." No indeed, Mother was not going for that! When the sun came up, you had your time in the bathroom to wash, brush your teeth, get dressed and eat your breakfast. All this had to be completed before Mother said, "It's time to go to Church children."

One by one we tossed the broken screen door open and journeyed by foot two blocks to the Church that sat on a hill. I remember my Father's distorted vision appearing in the torn screen shouting; "Yaw be good today." and he would then wave goodbye.

I do not know why my Dad did not join us for Church during those younger years. I do know that we could not stay home. My Mother was not falling for that! There was never an excuse good enough to give you a pass for not attending Church on the Lord's day.

I never read the Bible. I do remember when Easter and Christmas came around, I had to read a verse from the Bible. I understood enough to know that Jesus once existed because Pastor Burns told the entire Church that it was in the Bible. "If it's in the Bible, then it's true." he insisted.

Then there were programs like Mother's Day. My Mom dressed me up in my finest dress that was heavy starched and placed me in front of the congregation to sing: "I come to the garden alone. While the dew is still on the roses. And the voice I hear, falling on my ear, the song of God discloses."

Hmmm, it is strange that I remember that old song because I had to be about

8 years old, standing on stage, looking out over the congregation. I would glance at my Mother sitting on the front pew, and she would instruct me with her hands to stand up straight.

Theodore Burns, our Pastor was a short fat man, high yellow complexion, thick black glasses and partially bald. His beard was always raggedy, but his teeth were so white. After the song was over Pastor Burns would shout "Praise HIS name." and the congregation would yell amen! Mother would walk swiftly to usher me back to our seats, because the Pastor was about to bring the Word.

Pastor Burns would always preach about going up yonder. I did not want to go to this yonder! I did not know where this yonder was and I was not interested in this place yonder! I did not understand what he was talking about a great deal of the time. I would often look over at my younger siblings or other kids who were not listening either. They were playing with each other and some had fallen asleep.

Every Sunday he would make his voice do this growling noise, slowing lifting his head to the ceiling and shouting. "One day your goanna look for me and I'll be gone." I thought that Pastor Burns was a little strange. But then again, that could not be true because it only happened at the end of his sermons. What was so amazing is that the adults loved this. *"Why does Mother bring us here when the adults are the ones enjoying themselves."* I asked myself with my head down.

I did enjoy attending Church on the First Sunday of each month because it was Communion Sunday. The Deacons' wives were assigned special seats in the first two rolls of the sanctuary. On this particular Sunday, they all dressed in white clothing from head to toe. It was a beautiful sight but even more so was the entertainment that Sis. Hobbs provided.

Sis. Hobbs was a gray-haired old lady, squinty eyes, plump cheeks, thick lips, and she had a big rear end. Being the president over the other Deaconess, she took her job seriously! When giving direction to the two assigned Deaconess standing on each end of the table, she would throw her hand around as if she were directing a symphony. But the comedy was when she would throw her head backwards and forward. The funny thing was she looked like an inflated peacock and it tickled me so.

Now, when her head came forward, it signaled the Deaconess to lift the perfectly starched white cloth over the silver trays beneath it. The Deacons on the other hand were dressed sharp. They sported all black suits and wore pure white gloves on their hands. When the white cloth was removed off the silver trays, the Deacons moved in formation as they served the congregation.

The first tray offered tiny pieces of crackers which represented Jesus Christ's body and then miniature cups of grape juice represented HIS blood. Once everyone ate the crackers and sipped the grape juice, then the air was filled with singing.

"What a fellowship, what a joy divine, leaning on the everlasting arms; What a blessedness, what a peace is mine, leaning on the everlasting arms".

Pastor Burns would then charge the members to stand and greet each other while singing because it was the benediction.

"Leaning, leaning, safe and secure from all alarms; Leaning, leaning, leaning on the everlasting arms."

When I was ten years old, I was baptized. I saw other children of different ages doing it, so I wanted to get in the water too.

One of the Deacons would allow only one person at a time to enter the pool. Once you stepped into the cold water, Pastor Smith slowly walked toward you and stood by your side.

Now, I am freezing in this cold pool of water and wishing I had not decided to do this, but here I was. He folded my arms and said something about Jesus. Then he pushed me backwards in the water and quickly brought me back up. I was shivering while the church exploded with cheers and hand claps. The music from the organ was blasting and I was led out of the pool by another Deacon standing on the opposite side of the pool. He was grinning from ear to ear. "That wasn't as much fun as I thought it would be." I muttered to myself. I had to remember that this was Church, not the City pool.

Attending Sunday School, I did not want to learn about Jonah in the Whale because it did not make sense to me. *How could a man survives being inside a whale for 3 days and 3 nights?" I asked myself. And how could David who was small in stature defeat a giant?* Those stories were not true, and I did not care to hear them.

My spiritual growth did not get any better as the years passed.

I had a rebellious spirt and I did not even know it. At an early age, I became a puppet for the devil.

At 16 years old, I wanted a Birthday Party, but I did not get it. My Mom said we could not afford it. There were 7 more mouths to feed besides myself and even though my Dad was working, money was modest. Whenever we wanted something besides the essentials, Mother would always say: "Money don't grow on trees." I did not understand that either and felt that my parents would just make up excuses, so we would shut up! I did not shut up! I stomped around the table and I positioned myself in the dining room where my Mother could easily see my pitiful face.

A few minutes later she would say: "What's the matter with you girl?" *"I want to have a 16th Birthday Party Mom!"* I replied, sniffing, and my face distorted from trying to look as pitiful as I could. "We can't have a party so don't ask me again", she said. Her reply was not harsh but the only thing I understood was she said no.

I ran out of the house crying. All my friends had a Birthday Party when they turned 16, was spinning around in my head. I ran to the playground, crying and feeling so sad. I felt she did not want to understand it! It was my Birthday and that is all that mattered!!!

The more I sat alone on the playground, the more I became angry. I could not understand why my 16 Birthday was not important to her. Why couldn't she say' "You can have a small party or something?" Why? Tears flooded my face as I kicked old cans and whatever my foot met with.

I began to act out at home after that and was reprimanded repeatedly. I even started skipping classes, and the lying began. Whatever my Mother tried to tell me, I simply ignored. She saw that I was beginning to mature, and physically mature a little too much. Boys noticed too and started paying attention to me and I began to notice them.

I ignored the warnings of my mother concerning the opposite sex. I could never figure out how my Mother always sensed things. She would say, "if you play with fire Saundra, you'll get burned." I know she was only repeating something she heard. The more she said it, the more I ignored it. *Just some old saying!* I mumbled. At age 16, I thought I was grown but little did I know that a hard head would trigger a modification in my life sooner or later.

Chapter Two

18 years old

Two years passed and I was now a Senior in High School. My friends and I could not wait for Friday to come because it meant party time! Telephones began to buzz from house to house, each wanting to know the location of the party for that weekend.

In the 70's, bell bottom pants were the fashion, but I stitched mine own because my parents couldn't afford to purchase them at the department store. But I was just as fashionable as my girlfriends and the guys thought so too!

Just about every weekend, my best girl-friend, Dee Washington and I would meet at her house and go through clothing magazines. Dee had been my best friend since the second grade and there was absolutely nothing that we did not know about each other. Dee was gorgeous and exceptionally talented in music. She loved the piano and played very well. She was part African American and White. She had the most beautiful tan skin, with adorable thick black hair that hung to her lower back. She was 5'0" and I was only 4'8". Even though I was a few months older than she was, she would always call me the young one, because I was shorter than her. Hmmm, I guess that's why. But it was ok! Dee and I were like real blood sisters and I could share anything under the sun with her. Because she and I were popular with the boys, it was necessary for us to keep up with the latest fashion trend. I loved blue and Dee loved the color pea green. Every Thursday after school, we would write on pieces of paper, place it in a box, shake it and pulled out one piece. Written on the pieces of papers were either blue or pea green. Whichever color was pulled, we would wear that to the party. Our friends always commented on us dressing in the shame colors. It made us stand out and brought attention. This is what we wanted!

Even though this was my Senior year, I still had to attend Church on Sundays because Sargent Mom demanded it to be. But it was ok because I soon discovered that if I just obeyed her, then I could do what I wanted. I thought I was being crafty but brewing in the darkness, a trap was being prepared for me! *"If she only knew what I was doing, she'd beat the skin off my body!"* I thought.

School had been in session for only 2 months and I noticed that I was feeling tired all the time. I told Dee about it and she suggested I see the doctor and I did. Dr. Benson ran several tests as I waited patiently. There was no need to panic. I was sure, I had an allergy or something simple.

Dr. Benson walked back into my room with his head down looking at this piece of paper. He took a deep breath and handed it to me. *"Oh, a prescription for pills"* I thought to myself as I looked at the read.

As he sat down beside me, he informed me that I was 6 weeks pregnant! *"OMG, my Mom's goanna beat the skin off of me."* I uttered as fear rose in me like a Fire! My whole life changed in that moment. I fought to hold my composure until I left the Doctors office and I then had an out of body experience in the parking lot.

"OMG I'm in trouble" I whispered as tears flooded my face. I slowly sat down in the parking lot and screamed looking toward heaven. I had no concerns about who saw me or heard me. "No! this can't be happening to me now!" I shouted. I held my head with both hands and I just sat there crying hysterically.

While consumed in the news, I heard footsteps approaching. I did not move; I could not move. Soon I heard an elderly male voice quiver. "Are you ok Miss?", he asked.

I did not turn around, but I hurriedly wiped my face and awkwardly struggled to stand. *"Yes Sir, I'm ok Sir".* I said to end the conversation and I started walking. I could not go home. I did not want to see Dee. I did not know what to do but I had to keep moving. You would have thought I was lost because I roamed in unfamiliar neighborhoods for hours.

Even though people were peeping out their windows, there were grubby men staring at me as if I did not belong, I just kept moving. The only thing that made sense was I had to keep putting one foot in front of the other. I continued walking slowly until I found myself in a more familiar neighborhood. My house was only a block in front of me.

I stopped just to sit on old lady Webster's steps to rest, all the while looking at my house. It appeared as if everyone was home because the house was lit up and my parents' cars were parked in front.

I was sick to my stomach as tears flooded my face repeatedly. There was no turning back and there was no way out for me. Now all the lies I told, I could not take back and all the times I thought I had outwitted my parents was not funny anymore.

"Saundra, Saundra, is that you?" A small voice across the way reached my ear. I wiped my face quickly and turned to face Sis. Ruben, one of our Sunday School teachers. She would always hug me on Sundays after our class was over.

"Yes Sis. Ruben I am on my way home Sis. Ruben." I replied gasping for air.

I stood facing her for a quick second and turned to hide my face. I waved good-bye without looking at her because the tears would have revealed how I was feeling inside. And I did not want her to call my parents broadcasting that something was wrong before I could get there myself.

"Lord Jesus, please don't let her kill me today." I uttered as I took that first step toward the house. Of all the people to call on, I had the nerve to call on Jesus now that trouble was before me. I shook my head disgusted at myself.

With every other step I took, I inhaled a deep breath. I know I was just a block away from home, but it took forever to make it to the front door. The sounds of family chatter, movement of chairs on hardwood floors and pots and pans clanking in the kitchen sounded so beautiful to me like I have never known. *"How is it, that I missed this before?"* I muttered to myself. I took another deep breath and entered in the house with my head down.

Chapter Three

Worse day of my life

*A*s soon as I closed the front door behind me, my throat felt like a cement block was caught in it. I grabbed my throat and massaged it quickly as I heard my Father call to me. "Sister is that you?" My father's voice inquired. I stopped in my tracks. My heart was beating so fast, but I managed to clear my throat. *"Yes Sir."* I replied.

I did not want to go any further into the house, but my bones locked in place and I could not turn myself around to run away. Tears began to satiate my eyes and then cascade quickly down my cheeks. I could not concentrate on the tears because I was trying to control my breathing.

Suddenly this tall frame of a man met me in the hallway. I looked up at him briefly and dropped my head. I could not see my Dad distinctly, but I knew it was him. He quickly ran to me when he saw the tears on my face and grabbed me as if he were shielding me. I felt his love for me in that embrace.

We stood quietly in the hallway for a little while holding on to each other. He then lifted my face that was full of shame and fear and called my Mother as we walked in the living room.

Mother was in the washroom when I entered the house so she had no idea that I had come home. Dad and I was sat in the living room when Mother found us. First thing she said was "What's going on?" She looked at Dad and then at me. She saw my face and she kneeled beside me and put her arm around me. "What happened, are you ok?" She asked with the look of a loving Mom.

She always had that look, but I was too selfish to notice their love for me. All I could do was break down and cry because I knew I was about to break their hearts and I was going to die! Mom motioned for me to move over so she could sit beside me. "What is wrong, what happened? She asked. Now she is sitting 2 inches from me and my heart is sprinting so much that I feel like I could faint!!

I sat there because I had no place else to go. Mom on one side and Dad on the other. This was the moment of truth and I had to face it weather I wanted to or not.

Mother wiped my face with a handkerchief she removed from her apron and told me to talk.

I cried the entire time as I told my parents that I was 6 weeks pregnant. My mother began to cry, and my Dad lowered his head and cuddled his hands together.

They were devastated to say the least. Mom told me that she was disappointed in me but that she would be by my side. Dad told me he loved me and would also help with whatever I needed but he wanted to have a talk with my boyfriend. During this time, I had no idea that there were problems with my parent's marriage.

I was thankful my parents did not make me feel worse than I did. I believe God knew that I did not want to die. Under by breath I said: *"Thank you God."*

Now I had to tell my boyfriend. I decided that I would tell him the following weekend, but for now, I needed time to get myself together because I have been crying for hours.

My heart had been beating fast like a racehorse and I have just experienced the scariest moment in my life. I only hoped that I did not have to experience anymore hard times once I told my boyfriend. I was so foolish because I had no idea that hard times had not even begun for me and my young life.

On Monday, that next week, I informed my boyfriend Curtis that I was six weeks pregnant. Curtis Kennedy was 5'8" a sexy brown skin hunk that played football at our school. We had been dating since our Sophomore year and I really cared about him. He was happy about the news of me being pregnant. He walked around with his chest out while his friends celebrated with him. Of course, his buddies were cracking jokes about him being tied down and losing his freedom.

I did not like their jokes and I did not like my boyfriend forgetting me in that moment. What can I say, I am in this situation because of my hardhead! Later that evening, my boyfriend came to talk with my Dad in the backyard.

I do not know what they talked about, but I was troubled when he left our house without saying goodbye. I could only imagine that my Dad was stiff with him. My Dad was a quiet man, but when it came to his children, he would hurt you! So, I am positive that the conversation they had was not nice!

As my baby grew, my relationship with my boyfriend changed. Curtis was interested in other girls and I was left on the side lines to watch it all happening. I felt abandoned. Everything was becoming clear that I not only had to give birth, but I still had to raise our son. Months and months went by and my Curtis was slowly drifting away.

My classmates were all making plans to attend college or move out of town, but I had no future plans besides raising my little baby. Soon my boyfriend was completely out of the picture and reality was in my face.

He was so bold with this new relationship. He would flaunt his new girlfriend around our friends, not thinking about how it would make me feel. I learnt early how to swallow life's gigantic pills and put on a phony face to cover the pain inside.

I did not accomplish well in school, but I truly could have. When I consider the possibilities, I just shake my head. I could have been a teacher, singer, nurse, a news reporter, a high-ranking officer in the military or even an actor. My focus was on the wrong things. Being disobedient and a liar is a dreadful combination that would only bring about unhappy consequences.

I still had to attend church because I was living with my Mother. But even going to Church on Sundays felt like a wasted effort and a misuse of valuable time.

My family was talented and even I had something. I had the gift of writing poetry.

Poetry allowed me to escape from my own reality and the opportunity to travel to faraway places. It was my fantasy world where I could make all the rules and create the characters. There were no problems, but complete freedom to do whatever you wanted. I used to write love poem for different people. I treasured the challenge of creating expressions of love for others. I cherished it, but it did not generate money! I continued writing poetry until my son was born and then it was time to go to work.

Babies require many things and those things cost money. I was hired to work at the same place my Mother worked as an Aide. Being a teenage Mother, working and trying to party was a little much at times. My Mother was wonderful because she taught me everything about taking care of my son. I needed her and she was there for me.

Another year and half passed, and Mother started working two jobs after my parents divorced. She did not have time to sit down with each of my siblings and check their homework or just talk to see if they were having problems.

I think my Mom was too tired to even be concerned with those problems but rather she concentrated more with making sure we had a roof over our heads and food on the table.

Chapter Four

The Devil's Playground

*M*y girlfriend Dee and I had heard of this bar on the south side of town and that it was a nice place. So, we decided to go on Saturday night. The place was nice, and it was rocking. The music sounded great and it was packed. I sat there for a while looking around the place and tapping my fingers on top of the bar.

I was busy looking around the club and shocked that this place housed wall to wall people. Soon a young man approached me and offered to buy us a drink. I looked at Dee and she nodded to accept and that I did. He appeared to be a gentleman and he was nice looking as well. DC, a dark skin man with big eyes and thick lips. He was built better than superman and walked with confidence. We started dating and after a couple of weeks, he invited me to his church. *OMG here we go. "Should I go or not?"* I thought. I was about to tell him no when he appeared with beautiful flowers and begged me to go. Finally, I gave in and I attended Church with him.

Even before we entered his Church, you could feel the vibration from the inside on the outside. *"What is going on up in here?"* I thought. I was shocked because I had never experienced anything like this. People in the choir stand leaping into the air, people running up and down the aisles, some crying, hands raised in the air and music blasting so loud as to bust the windows out.

I was really scared. He saw the expression on my face and gently took my hand and smiled. I felt better as I was moving around in my seat trying not to miss anything that was going on.

The preacher stepped to the pulpit and raised his hands. Everything became silent except for a few softer 'Thank you Jesus" across the sanctuary. It was preaching time and I really did not want to hear what he was going to say. Suddenly this thunderous voice rolled jumped out of his mouth and he began to sing "Pass Me Not".

I watched in amazement as I listened to the song and watched him sing with his eyes closed and his head back. Slowly more voices chimed in and it was so sweet. Even I mumbled a few words as I had heard this song at my church many times.

I could tell the Pastor was sincere and it touched me. I thought about it making me feel some kind of way. I could not help it for it was powerful. The atmosphere was electric. Surely nothing like I had ever experienced. My eyes became watery as I reasoned within myself the height of service in this Church. There's no denying that I felt something and soon my feet moved about the wooden floor.

"Pass Me Not is a powerful song." I thought to myself. I thought about my sons' father and how he decided to pass us by. How my Son will feel one day knowing he was thrown away. The song says: While on others thou

art calling, do not pass me by. I know this is a Church song, but I thought it was more fitting for my personal life and my situation. I shook my head and returned to the service.

The Pastor began to preach with such power and animation. I was 100% caught up with his intense preaching. I did not move an inch. He screamed: "You need to get your house in order! Because God is coming back for a Church without a spot or wrinkle." He shouted.

I did not understand that remark. *"There are so many Churches in the USA not to mention the thousands and thousands of Churches in the world."* I quietly thought. *"Why would God only come after a Church? Does that mean only one Church in the entire world?"* I wrestled within my mind.

After service, I asked my boyfriend DC to explain what the Pastor meant when he said: "God is coming for a Church." He explained that the Church represents individual people. *"Hmmm, that was interesting."* I thought to myself.

I continued to attend Church with DC and I must admit that I heard a lot of interesting things. Still I was reluctant to accept some of it, well most of it! Even more so since my relationship ended after a few months. We remained friends though and that was nice. Our friendship was safe, but the world was calling me back and I did not hesitate to return to it.

One date took me to a movie and another to dinner, not really having a meaningful relationship. Soon I was introduced to Marijuana. I was partying even more, smoking weed, puffing cigarettes, drinking, working and trying to be a Mom.

I was pathetic but Dee and other friends kept telling me that I was young and that I should have all my fun right now. So, when I began to feel ashamed of my actions, I reasoned that I was still a young woman and that I should enjoy my youth while I could. After all, I really enjoyed the drugs, alcohol, and smoking cigarettes.

I moved around a lot and was often behind in my utilities. I was completely immature. I just could not get myself together and the people that was in my circle was just like me. I can hear my Dad say: "Birds of a feather flock together. Yeah, that was me and my friends.

Even though I wrestled with my own conscience, there was yet another voice communicating with me to **STOP**. I was in a battle that I could not conquer. I was being yanked from the left to the right! I would find myself always crying. Crying for answers that were beyond my reach!

As years passed, it became clear that my actions were not what I wanted for myself. There were days when my friends would come by and I really did not want to see them. Dee would get angry with me because she felt that I was snubbing her. Maybe I was but I was fighting a battle that she knew nothing about.

I knew that if I ever told her that I was trying to change my lifestyle, she would have a fit. I mean, she loved the parties as much as I if not more and I could not bring myself to have that conversation. I cannot even imagine what that conversation would be like.

There were occasions when my friends informed me that a big party was happening on the following weekend and it did not excite me. But I acted as if I was excited just to save face. I mean, we have been partying for years and to tell them I did not want to party with them anymore would be a disaster.

Even though there was a tiny voice whispering to: **STOP**, I did not know how to stop. Besides, I was too ashamed and afraid to ask for help from someone outside our circle. "Who would care? Who would have time for me? How could I be sure that their advice was genuine?" I whispered to myself and threw the idea back in the closet and slammed the door.

Chapter Five

Walking In Shame

*T*hroughout the year, Holidays would come, and I became ashamed to run into old classmates. I felt shame because they went on to college and was doing great things. I absolutely did not want them to know what I was doing, in fear of being judged. On the outside I was still petite and cute. Well to be honest, I learned how to use makeup that brought my eyes back to life and a youthful look to my skin.

Why did it feel like I was carrying around a cement boulder on my back? I wondered. Seeing my classmates looking good and accomplishing their goals made me drop my head in shame.

Several months later, I bumped into one of my classmates at the grocery store. Carl Hunter had become a Deacon at his Father's church. He was so happy to see me and we talked for a long time. Carl was one of those guys that would make a good husband. He was tall, soft spoken and caring. The problem I had with Carl was he was too stiff. He did not know how to have fun and his Dad had a grip on him like a bite from a pit bull. I now think that was a good thing. He looked great and his laughter was infectious. When I reminisce about that day, I believe my talk with him stirred something within me.

He did not look at me as if he were better than I. He was respectful, and I knew what he shared with me was sincere. I left that conversation with Carl, tears flowing down my face and admitting that I was living in hell and the devil was the landlord.

I remember crying in my bedroom while looking at myself in the mirror. "You need help!" I told myself. Without any doubt, the moment of truth welled up in me. But that voice counter punched me by reminding me to enjoy my youth. Once again, I returned to the world. My friends would tell me the same old stuff about living for the weekend but even though I was ready to walk away, I didn't walk away. The struggle was real, and I did not know which way to turn.

A few years later on a Saturday after Thanksgiving, I ran an errand with my girl-friend Dee for her Mother. When we returned to her Mother's house, she asked me to enter the home with her and I did. I spoke loudly to her family so they could hear me in the back, and I sat down on the couch across from this lady. She looked at me and smiled and I smiled back. Her face was so lovely, and she appeared to be genuinely nice.

My girlfriend went to the back of the house where her Mother was resting without speaking to this lady. *"Now I know my Mother would kill me if I ever disrespected another adult."* I whispered to myself. I slouched down on the couch facing the lady wonder-ing what to say.

She nodded her head and smiled at me again and I smiled back. I knew I had already smiled but maybe this was some grownup's way of communicating. She then learned toward me and with a stern look she said: "Repent child!" I quickly leaned back against the couch. I could feel my eyebrows peak and my eyes opened wide. *"Ok, now what is going on?"* I asked myself all the while looking at this woman. She gazed at me for a few minutes and her smile returned.

She quickly stood up, leaned over and looked down the hallway where everyone else was and said her goodbyes to my girlfriends' family. She then took two steps toward me, stooped over, crossed both hands in front of her and whispered. "You can't do what other people do!"

I pushed myself back even further into the couch as if I were trying to push a hole through it! This lady frightened me! She reached in her purse, pulled out a Bible and waved it in the air and left with her head in the air.

I think I had a meltdown as I sat there looking at the wall, hoping she had not forgotten something and needed to return. *"Oh God!"* I whispered! I quickly looked behind me toward the front door and then leaned forward to see if Dee was on her way. I was ready to go and I wanted to go now! I sat there breathing rapidly and looking all around wondering if I was tripping.

A few minutes passed and Dee ran toward me smiling. 'You ready girl?" she asked. *"Yep, let's go!"* I responded. I immediately stood but I was shaken for a few minutes. We left her Mom's house with my hands wrapped around my waist as I walked to the vehicle. I thought it best to look all around me just in case that woman didn't pop up in my face again. "Come on girl" Dee shouted. I took a deep breath and jumped in the car. We drove off.

I never told Dee about that incident. Well, she does drugs too and I did not want her telling our friends that I was tripping at her Mother's house. *"Was I tripping or was she real?"* I wondered to myself.

I did not like that experience and I thought about what she said to me. "You can't do what other people do!" *I felt that in my soul!.* "I whispered." *"How does she know what I'm doing? How does she know me? What other people is she talking about and is she spy-*

ing on me and why?" These thoughts bobbled around in my mind.

People become alcoholics because they drink too much, and I could be a drug addict because I do drugs and sometimes too much." I thought to myself. I glanced over at my girlfriend who was singing a song and driving. I knew I had to keep my mouth shut about this, so I rested my head back on the headrest. *"That makes the second time someone has spoken to me about my life."* I thought.

I closed my eyes as we drove down the freeway and thought *"Somebody is watching me, and I don't know why?"* This is a bad feeling.

Chapter Six

25 Years Old

*A*s I became older, life challenged me like you wouldn't believe. It did not get easier for me but harder. On more than too many occasions I found that the storms were too strong for me. *"How many times will Mother allow me to return home without asking me questions that I really didn't want to share with her."* I pondered. If she knew the truth, it would hurt her. I had to figure things out, so I decided to help myself.

"What was I to do? Where was I to go? Who would help me with these problems?" I asked myself.

I had to be honest with myself and not point the finger at anyone else. "I whispered." There was no other way but to admit that I drank too much and smoked too much weed. Oh and of course the partying had to cease as well as smoking. As a Mother I should not be living and acting like an overaged teenager.

I sat on my bed and covered my face with my pillow. After many relationships of falling in and out of love or what I thought was love, I did not realize that I was still a little girl desiring to be loved and needing to be important to somebody.

I allowed men to treat me less than my worth. I allowed the abuse from some men in exchange to feel love. I neglected the responsibility of my son at times just to drink and party. It is one thing to have others tell you about yourself, but to be critically honest with oneself is worse.

Chapter Seven

A Change Has To Come

I was raised in church, but I did not have a relationship with God. The world looked shinny and glamorous and had more to offer. I figured I would give God that one day out of the week and put as little money as I could in the offering. You know just enough without making a sacrifice. I thought I was so smart, but someone was watching EVERYTHING I did!

From relationship to relationship, year after year, I continued to acknowledge God once a week. This is when my relationship (if I had one at the time) was going well. But when things began to fall apart and got rocky, then and only then would I cry out to HIM. How foolish and self-center I was!

Not having the good sense to think that

- if my body became seriously ill, none of my friends or lovers could cure me.
- if I lost a limb, none of my friends or lovers could replace it.
- If I lost my sight, not one of my friends or lovers could heal me.

Yet they took center stage in my life before God! Once again, I found myself alone. I was thankful to have my son in my life. He needed me and he was worth me making a lifestyle change.

One Tuesday I believe it was, I decided to turn on the Gospel channel. A Minister was preaching about freely making a choice for a new life. He asked the audience if they were tired of failure, tired of feeling all alone and tired of things not going right in their lives.

He continued to say: "If you need healing in your mind, and your body, that Jesus was the answer for that."

As he walked closer to the camera, I felt he was looking at me and I took a few steps closer to the TV. "Are you ready my Sister for

God to remove that cement boulder that's been on your back?"

My mouth flew opened and again, this river of tears flooded my face. I felt myself slowly falling to my knees as I kept my eyes on this man. Before I knew what I was doing, I said yes with all my strength and I repeated it again. "Yes!"

The Minister instructed the TV audience to touch the screen so we would all be on one accord and I did. He asked me to confess with my mouth that I was a sinner and I did. He asked everyone if they believed that Christ died on the cross and I said yes. He walked closer to the camera and asked: "Are you now willing to surrender your life to Jesus?" Again, I said, "Yes." while letting the tears flood my face.

The Minister continued sharing that Jesus voluntarily gave HIS life for my sins. I had to run and get the dictionary because I was not really sure what SIN meant. "My wrongdoings, wickedness or crimes." I whispered. There was another man sitting on stage with the Minister. He held an open Bible and stood as he spoke these words:

"but HE was wounded for our transgressions, he was bruised for our iniquities; the chastisement of our peace was upon him; and with his stripes we are healed" Isaiah 53:5."

I sat on my bed, reaching for my tablet. I kept repeating the scripture so I would not forget it.

Isaiah 53:5. "Finally I found it on my tablet, but I needed to read with understanding from my sisters easy to read Bible and there it was' I said.".

"but HE was wounded (injured) for our transgressions (wrongdoings), he was bruised (hurt) for our iniquities (sins); the chastisement (punishment) of our peace was upon him; and with his stripes (whip lash on his back) we are healed."

"Could I do that? Could I be crucified for someone else?" I softly whispered. I sat at the end of my bed trying to grasp this Jesus. This was a challenge as I tried to comprehend this kind of love.

Jesus died for me? "I questioned". The relationships I engaged in, never, not once did someone make a sacrifice for me, yet they said I Love You. I walked to the window and glided the curtains and sheers away to clear the view of a sunset. A battle of understanding was going on in my mind, yet there was still another battle occurring in my ear.

"Don't worry yourself about that Jesus, you have your entire life to think about HIM." the voice shouted. I had to shake my head to rid the negativity that filled my ear and I fell willingly to my knees. I did not know how to approach God or what to say about all of this. I remained there for a while, feeling incredibly sad.

Chapter Eight

The Turn Around

Later that week, Dee called asking why we had not been spending time together. She sounded a little sour, but I knew we needed to chat.

I suggested that we meet around 7pm at her parents and she agreed. I'm not one to pray but I knew meeting her would be different so as I stepped to the front and whispered; *"God, I need to talk to my friend and I need your help with that. Thank you."* I took a deep breath and knocked on her door.

The door opened and my girlfriend stood smiling at me. "Well hello friend!" she yelled and swung the screen door open for me." "Hello" I said" and gave her a hug.

We sat down at the dining room table and she wasted no time to tell me about an upcoming party. I sat there knowing that I was not about to go back to the streets. I was truly sick of it! I was tired of it and I wanted something much fulfilling for myself.

She noticed that I was not present or really listening, so she stopped talking abruptly and looked at me as if I were an alien.

I coupled my face with my hands for a minute and then looked at my friend. *"I've been on this whirlwind of partying, sleeping around and taking drugs for years. I just cannot do it anymore."* I said looking at her through watery eyes.

She rolled her head in a circle and stopped to glare at me. "What is your problem?" she asked sharply. "Where is my girlfriend that likes to party hardy?" she shouted. *"I'm tired Dee. I'm tired of being tired and I'm not happy."* I replied. "I don't understand what your problem is. "We are young women who love the bars and we should be enjoying ourselves girl!" she shouted.

It was evident that I needed to try another way to make her understand. I sat straight up and reached for her hand. *"You and I have been friends since we were born. We've done a lot of things good and we've done a lot of things that weren't good."* I said while looking at her. She immediately withdrew her hand from mine. "So you no longer apart of the clique?" She shouted again and with anger!

I felt something, like a boldness or courage came over me. *"Why are you shouting at me?* I asked and frowned at her. "You sound like you're breaking up with me or something." she stuttered. I sat there thinking about what she just said. "Well, I'm no longer going to parties and sleeping around." I said.

"We've done those things for so many years and I'm ashamed of myself. I don't want it anymore." I said with tears in my eyes. She sat there glaring at me as if I were talking a foreign language to her.

I could tell that it did not matter what I tried to share with her, the only thing that mattered was I Wasn't Going to Party With Her Anymore! Although it hurt my heart to leave her angry with me, I only hoped that one day she would understand. I left my girl-friend's house with our friendship uncertain and a sad heart crying yet rejoicing too. It was the first step to my new life.

Chapter Nine

Something New

*I*found myself talking to a God that I had never met I even prayed for my friends and with hope this new life would be all the Minister said it would be. I started watching him regularly because I was desperate. I wanted to learn more.

I had problems understanding a lot of the scriptures, but the Minister said to keep reading because God would give me the understanding.

Ephesians 1:17 says: "That the God of our Lord Jesus Christ, the Father of glory, may give unto you the spirit

of wisdom and revelation in the knowledge of him."

On Wednesdays, I began attending Bible Study at our Church and I stopped drinking and drug usage. It was not easy returning to the Church because I knew people had heard and witnessed me running with the wrong people. But I had to hang my head down and walk in the shame. Some of them whispered as I walked by and there were others who rolled their eyes at me, but I had to endure like Jesus endured on the cross. I knew this was all a part of my change.

Those Church members that treated me like I had no business attending Bible Study, made me cry. But a voice whispered to me. "Pray for them." I was not always a bad girl, but these same Church folks have known me since I was born, yet they treated me like dirt.

I think this was the most undesirable kind of hurt I could ever experience. I thought the Church was a place for the downtrodden, the lost, and sinners like me. I thought the Church that I attended so much of my life would embrace a troubled soul, but it didn't. The older Church members who never in

their lives smoked a joint, puffed on cigarettes, had several lovers, drank MD 20/20, or
Gin & 7, treated me with no LOVE. *"What
was I to do? Should I sit with them or run?"* I
muttered to myself.

I thought about it and I remember reading in the Bible about forgiveness.

> **Colossians 3:13 "Forbearing one
> another, and forgiving one another,
> if any man have a quarrel against
> any; even as Christ forgave you, so
> also do ye."**

I had to forgive them because Christ said
in HIS word to forgive. I have forgiven and I
prayed for them.

Something wonderful was happening to
me but I had to have major surgery. The kind
of surgery that would give me a new way of
thinking, a new way of walking, and a new
way of talking.

> **Romans 12:2 "And do not be
> conformed to this world, but be
> transformed by the renewing of
> your mind, that you may prove**

what *is* that good and acceptable and perfect will of God.

HIS will is what I needed. I had lived my life doing things against my parents will and I did things my way. But I knew I was ready for a new way of living and I was on the path to get it.

Little did the Church members know but something was moving on the inside of me. I felt it and soon the dirt and grime of that old life slowly fell off me. This God that I had never met welcomed me with HIS arms wide open. I was now ready to be presented as a new creature of Christ Jesus!

2 Corinthians 5:17 "Therefore if any man be in Christ, he is a new creature; old things are passed away; behold, all things are become new."

My God began shifting things, reshaping me, throwing away this and replacing it with that. HE was filling me with substance and adding richness to my life. My God was remolding me and bringing forth a new Saundra! Hallelujah!

When I think of the many moments I lived dangerously and not once did I pray. He protected me from dangers seen and unseen and I never said Thank You! Like my parents, Jesus never disowned me or cast me aside, but HE forgave me and embraced me. Although HE was disappointed in me, HE loved me enough to hold death in its place.

As I write to you today, I want to cry. I feel like screaming! Not because I am angry, but because I should not be writing this book. When I look back at all those years that I ran on the playground of a reckless life, I should have been dead and gone. But then something within me whispers: "Amazing Grace, how sweet the sound. That saved a wretch like me. I once was lost but now am found, I was blind but now I see." Praise God!

I am not here today because I went to the alter at the Church and rededicated my life to Christ. It was HIS mercy (compassion) and grace (unmerited favor) toward me. I had to surrender **my will** and turn away from everything that was the opposite of what God required of me. It is what HE requires of everyone regardless of your gender, your age, your nationality or social status.

He has the right to have requirements because HE died for us and HE is GOD! HE is the Jehovah Jira; the one that provides for you. HE is Adoniah; HE is Lord, Master.

.

John 3:16: "For God so loved the world, that HE gave HIS only begotten son, that whoever believes in HIM should not perish but have everlasting life."

Some will have a problem with what I am sharing, because they want their cake and ice cream too. We only want to give God what we want to give HIM, but HE is the MASTER and HE **will not** accept that. HE wants 100% of you. 991/2% won't do.

The sacrifices I made to walk with JESUS was nothing compared to HIM dying on the cross for my sins. I cannot imagine the agony he suffered hanging on that cross when HE could have come down by himself. But HE decided to die, for it was the only way that you and I could be saved. I cannot imagine JESUS who was innocent of any wrong doings, being spit at, whipped, a crown of thorns placed on HIS head, being pierced with a sword and anguished for someone like me. I am not worthy of HIS love.

We cannot live how we want to live and expect to go to heaven. In other words, we cannot be a part of the world and go to heaven. We must turn from the world and live every day for JESUS. Our heart, our mind, our spirit must line up with HIM. We must surrender our will, our way of life, our hopes, our dreams, and our families.

> **"I John 2: 15-17 "Do not love the world or the things in the world. If anyone loves the world, the love of the Father is not in him. For all that is in the world, the lust of the flesh, the lust of the eyes, and the pride of life is not of the Father but is of the world. And the world is passing away, and the lust of it; but he who does the will of God abides forever."**

> **Ephesians 4:23-24 "And be renewed in the spirit of your mind; And that ye put on the new man, which after**

God is created in righteousness and true holiness."

Right now, there may people you know, they may be complete strangers, but it's obvious they are having a rough time. You see them but you turn your head. You don't offer them a few dollars but forget them as soon as you pass them by because they're dirty or beneath you. You don't offer a quiet prayer while passing by cause that might seem stupid. But one of the many wonderful things about Jesus is this, HE's not afraid to get HIS hands dirty. He is not afraid to come in the midst of his children, wash them, and place their feet on a solid path. I am so thankful that God loved me enough to say: "Daughter rise and come unto me and rest." Hallelujah!"

I am grateful that my eyes are open. Finally, I understand that without JESUS, I would not be able to walk without assistance from JESUS holding my hand. I realize that without JESUS, I can do nothing. Some people honestly believe that the time clock wakes them up but it does not. God's grace that allows you to open your eyes. It is his mercy and grace that allows you see, hear, breath and move.

> **Acts 17:28 NKJV "For in <u>Him</u> we live and move and have our being, as also some of your own poets have said, 'For we are also His offspring.'**

God will never force himself on you. HE will not make you choose HIM over anything. You must come to HIM with a willing heart. HE has given us free will.

I realize that the relationships I so willingly entered into were temporary. What I love about God is HE is FOREVER! I am glad that I get all of HIM and not a small part of HIM. Unlike us, God does not half step. HE lovingly gives us HIS all.

I had to show God that I was willing to try HIS way! I had to say NO to the old life I was living. I had to literally turn my back to it. To prove that I wanted HIM in my life required me to act. I had to lay down my life just as HE did for me. I did not die on the cross, but I died to the ways of this world.

> **Galatians 2:20: "I have been crucified with Christ, it is no longer I who**

**lives, but Christ lives in me, and the
life which I now live in the flesh I live
by faith in the Son of God, who loved
me and gave Himself for me. (nkjv)**

It sounds easy but it was not. The devil
was moving in on me and as time went on,
I had my battles to deal with. Not just with
men I had been involved with, but family
things as well! You see the devil does not care
who he hurts or uses.

**John 10:10 (nkjv) "The thief does
not come except to steal, and to kill,
and to destroy. I (Jesus) have come
that they may have life, and they may
have it more abundantly."**

If the devil can find a tiny crack in your
armor, (your mind, your heart, your ears) he
will weasel his way in. The devil will send
recruiters in your life. He will send people
that appear to be nice and appear to make
you think they're your friend. Even some who
attend church are sent to fool you and to pull
you away from the great plans that God has
for you. We think JESUS hates us and HE
does not want us to have fun. But this untrue.

> **Jeremiah 29:11 "For I know the plans I have for you; declares the Lord, "plans to prosper you and not to harm you, plans to give you hope and a future." The church is a revival kit.**

It is up to us to be educated in the Word of God, so we do not get caught up in the snares of the devil. It is vital that you are under the leadership of a Pastor and one that is preaching the Word of God boldy. The church is survival kit!

There were times I just could not get myself out of the mix of things, because I kept trying to give God a hand. What I needed to do was move out of the way and let God be God!

Chapter Ten

Now I See

- How many times did I make God cry?
- How many broken promises did I make?
- How many times did I break HIS heart?
- How many days went by and I never not once acknowledged HIM.
- How many times did I not thank him for food on my table and a roof over my head? How many?
- How many times I sat in Church with a man on my mind instead of listening to what saith the Lord?
- How many times did HE watch me put others before HIM?
- How many times did I steal from HIM by not paying my tithes?

- How many times was I lazy to kneel and pray?
- How many times did I check Facebook while the Pastor was preaching?
- How many times was I texting in Church and Bible Study?
- How many times did I inhale and exhale for granted?

*T*he Love that I wanted and needed so badly was there the entire time. On too many occasions HE rocked me to sleep and wiped the tears from my face. HE gently pulled the covers over me and stood guard at my front door. Standing in the shadows of my life, HE quietly watched me run from one relationship to another. Patiently HE waited for me to acknowledge HIM.

So many times, I was too high and too drunk to drive home, but it was the hand of GOD that guided me to safety.

Daily HE provided for me, comforted me, held my broken heart in HIS hands and opened my eyes to a new day. JESUS, there is none like HIM. Halleujah!

Luke 1:37 "For with God nothing will be impossible."

I understand that denying those desires and old habits can be difficult for you to handle alone but nothing is impossible for GOD! Absolutely nothing!

Everything I was doing in the dark and behind my parents back, was not hidden from GOD! I thought I was so clever, but I was only fooling myself. There is not one secret on this planet that HE is not aware of.

Luke 12:2-3 "For there is nothing covered that will not be revealed, nor hidden that will not be known. Therefore, whatever you have spoken in the dark will be heard in the light, and what you have spoken in the ear in inner rooms will be proclaimed on the housetops."

You can decide right now to accept JESUS as your personal Savior.

Revelation 3:20 (nkjv) "Behold, I stand at the door and knock. If anyone hears my voice and opens the door, I will come in to him and dine with him and he with me."

Knock knock! He's knocking at the door of your heart at this very moment. Do you hear HIM? How many times has he knocked and you didn't answer? How many more times will you ignore HIS call?

I promise you as soon as you turn your back to the world, JESUS will step in and make you a new creature like HE did with me."

If you are hungry for a change in your life, you can choose JESUS right where you are. JESUS has been planning a beautiful life for you before you even existed.

> **Jeremiah 1:5 (nkjv) "Before I formed you in the womb, I knew you; Before you were born, I sanctified you; I ordained you a prophet to the nations."**

HE is waiting for you. HE has been preparing blessings and opportunities for you since the beginning of time.

> **Psalms 8: 4-8 (nkjv) "What is man that You are mindful of him, And the son of man that You visit him? For You have made him a little lower than**

the angels, And You have crowned him with glory and honor. You have made him to have dominion over the works of Your hands; You have put all things under his feet, All sheep and oxen even the beast of the field, The birds of the air, And the fish of the sea that pass through the paths of seas."

This is so powerful! Who are we (humans) that Jesus is so mindful of us? Mindful = watchful, attentive or thoughtful. Have you ever though to ask that question? Who am I? Who are you, that the Creator of heaven and earth is mindful of your everyday life? JESUS, who died on calvary and rose in three days is mindful of your dreams, goals, and desires? YOU really matter to HIM!

He knows you better than you know yourself. He has seen your struggles and wants to help you. If the world, so called friends and my family divorce me, I am determined to follow JESUS. I have forgiven those who abused me, that hated me, talked about me and made fun of me. And you know what, it's because JESUS forgave me too.

As I sit at my desk gazing out my bedroom window, I feel the love of God in my heart. I am not what I used to be! Hallelujah!

Philippians 3:14 (nkjv) "I press toward the mark for the prize of the high calling of GOD in CHRIST JESUS.

When I think about HIS love, it amazes me so. I know today that HE walks with me and talks with me. I understand that HE was loving enough to give me a road map to follow through HIS word. I understand that there is no battle or situation too difficult for HIM.

The blinds have been removed from my eyes and I now see clearly the path that HE has placed before me. There is a finish line waiting for me to cross and I am determined to complete the race! I know that I am loved in a way that no one else has ever cared or loved me.

I am so grateful that HE WAITED FOR ME, to wake up and choose HIM!

THE END